Robin Ray's Music Quiz

Robin Ray's Music Quiz

B.T. BATSFORD LTD · LONDON

First published 1978
© Robin Ray 1978

Designed by Alan Hamp

Filmset in 'Monophoto' Photina by
Servis Filmsetting Ltd, Manchester

Printed in Great Britain by
The Anchor Press Ltd, Tiptree, Essex
for the Publishers B.T. Batsford Ltd
4 Fitzhardinge Street, London W1H 0AH

ISBN 0 7134 1492 8

Introduction

One way or another I feel I have been taking part in quizzes all my life. From my earliest days in school, squirming in my seat at the desk, my hand raised high in proud delight in knowing the answer to a question from the teacher to the class; at home, when my father would offer 'handsome cash prizes' (you could win up to half-a-crown!) if you could tell him who played opposite Chester Morris in *Blind Alley*; and later, on television and radio, compiling questions for programmes like *The Movie Quiz* or answering them on the ever popular *Face the Music*. I must admit that I never imagined earning my living, or at least part of it, merely by doing in public the very things that gave me pleasure in private, and I am grateful for such a happy coincidence; it made compiling this book both easy and enjoyable.

Why, I wonder, do so many people enjoy taking part in a quiz? I think there are three main reasons: when you know the answer it's rewarding to show off and impress your friends (or rivals); if you don't know the answer you have an opportunity to learn something new in a fairly painless way; and finally it's nice to win — especially a prize. I can't offer you the last of these benefits, but I do hope you'll gain something of the first two.

Although, to the best of my knowledge, I have dreamed up most of the questions in this book myself I did find it necessary to rely on some old friends for detailed confirmation of both questions and answers, and I would like to acknowledge with gratitude the help these old friends gave me from my library shelves: *The Oxford Companion To Music* — Scholes (Oxford University Press), *Collins Encyclopedia Of Music* — Sir Jack Westrup and F.Ll. Harrison, revised by Conrad Wilson (Collins), *The Encyclopedia of Dance and Ballet* — Edited by Mary Clarke and David Vaughan (Pitman), *Kobbe's Complete Opera Book* — Edited and Revised by the Earl of Harewood (Putnam), *The Encyclopedia Of Opera* — Edited by Leslie Orrey and Gilbert Chase (Pitman), *Lexicon Of Musical Invective* — Nicolas Slonimsky (University Of Washington Press), *Great Composers Through The Eyes Of Their Contemporaries* — Edited by Otto Zoff (E.P. Dutton & Co., New York), and *The Guinness Book Of Music Facts and Feats* — Robert and Celia Dearling and Brian Rust (Guinness Superlatives, Ltd) as well as all the countless writers of books and record sleeve notes and concert programmes that have contributed to my knowledge over the years.

I would also like to thank Archivo Storico Ricordi, Sophie Baker, Clive Barda, Peter Bartok, Bibliothèque de Conservatoire, Boosey and Hawkes Ltd, Allan Chapelow, Columbia Warner Distributors Ltd, Contemporary Films Ltd, Decca Record Company, Deutsche Gramophon, EMI, David Farrell, Hakim Brothers, Harold Holt, Ibbs and Tillett, Library of Congress (The Elizabeth Sprague Coolidge Foundation Collection and the Gertrude

Clarke Whittall Foundation Collection), London Films, Suzie Maeder, Mansell Collection, Norman McCann, MGM Pictures, National Film Archive, National Portrait Gallery, Nebelspalter, Philips, Photographie Giraudon (Collection M Pincherle), Polydor, Popperfoto, Radio Times Hulton Picture Library, Rank Film Distributors Ltd, RCA Records, Staatsbibliothek Preussischer Berlin, 20th Century-Fox, and United Artists Corporation Ltd, for the use of various pictures, prints and stills; and Annette Brown for her imagination in tracing them and diligence in looking them out.

I would like to end these acknowledgments with a special word of thanks to Dr Stanley Sadie who very kindly acted as a musical guinea pig, answering and checking my questions from my own wild manuscript — a difficult task for which I am most grateful.

The quiz falls roughly into four sections. The first of these is intended as a 'warm up' for what comes later, a rough equivalent of the exercises that an instrumentalist might run through before playing at a concert. The other sections are intended to be harder — the last hardest of all. The whole book contains a total of 379 questions and if all are answered correctly they are worth a grand total of 545 marks. For those who bravely soldier on to the end here is a rough guide as to how you rate:

Over 500	Genius. Take up directorship of La Scala Milan at once!
450 to 500	A brilliant score. You are well qualified to run a major classical record company or act as guest conductor for the New York Philharmonic Orchestra.
350 to 450	Good. A little to learn still, but you are entitled to a generous salary as adviser to the Head Librarian at the British Broadcasting Corporation.
250 to 350	Average. A respectable job with a small concert agency or music publisher.
150 to 250	Fair. Go to work in a record shop with a limited classical section, and try to improve *your* knowledge and *their* stock!
50 to 150	Poor. Buy a record!
1 to 50	Bad. Set out the chairs and music stands for the Paris Conservatoire and do try not to fall over them!

Pencils and papers ready —
Good luck —

Robin Ray

SECTION ONE

One

Identify the following composers from their portraits below. (One mark for each, maximum score 10)
For the answers please turn to the end of the book

1

2

3

4

5

6

7

8

9

10

10

Two

The following are **potted plots of ten well-known operas**. Name the opera and composer in each case. (One mark for each, maximum score 20)

1 A poet, a painter, a philosopher and a musician are living in the Latin Quarter in Paris in about 1830. Two of them have girl friends, one of whom dies.

2 In Egypt a Prince frees a Queen's daughter with the aid of an enchanted instrument.

3 We are in and around Paris. A young man falls in love with a courtesan. The boy's father begs her to give him up to avoid a family scandal. Having made the sacrifice she dies.

4 During the reign of the Empress Maria Theresa, in Vienna, a young man of seventeen is in love with a Princess, who is considerably older than he. Later he falls in love with a pretty young girl who has already been promised to a crude nobleman in need of some money. The Princess realises she cannot hold her lover any longer and graciously accepts the young couple's happiness together.

5 During the French wars of 1797 a young sailor on board H.M.S. *Indomitable* unwittingly becomes the enemy of an evil Master-at-Arms. The boy accidentally kills his persecutor, and is hanged.

6 It is about 1820 in Seville, Spain, when a soldier falls in love with an employee in a cigarette factory. When she transfers her affections to a bull fighter, the soldier murders her.

7 We are still near Seville, but this time it is the eighteenth century. A faithful wife disguises herself as a man in order to free her husband from prison.

8 In Charleston, South Carolina, USA, is a Negro tenement called Catfish Row. A tough stevedore is killed by a cripple over a girl, who subsequently takes dope and leaves South Carolina for New York.

9 In Nuremberg in the middle of the sixteenth century a Franconian knight sings a song at a midsummer festival, winning both a prize and a bride.

10 It is Easter day in a village in Sicily. A young soldier has been conducting a love affair with the wife of the village teamster. On hearing of the relationship from a village girl the husband kills the soldier in a knife fight.

Three

The following actors played **composers in film biographies**. Identify actor, composer, and title of film. (One mark for each, maximum score 30)

1

2

3

4

5

6

7

8

9

10

Four

Give the approximate **English equivalent of the following musical terms.**
(One mark for each, maximum score 10)

1 Mezza voce

6 Presto

2 Lento

7 Poco

3 Diminuendo

8 Arpeggio

4 Glissando

9 Segue

5 Staccato

10 Bravura

Five

A mixed bag of **well-known faces to identify**. (One mark for each, maximum score 10)

1

2

3

4

5

6

7

8

9

10

Six

Variations on or arrangements of the works of other composers. Who was responsible? (One mark for each, maximum score 10)

1 Orchestral transcription of Musorgsky's *Pictures At An Exhibition*.

2 Variations on a theme of Corelli, Opus 42.

3 Variations on a theme of Paganini, Opus 35.

4 Symphonic Metamorphoses of Themes of Weber.

5 Variations on a theme of Frank Bridge.

6 Concert paraphrase of themes from Verdi's *Rigoletto*.

7 Transcription for piano solo of the Chaconne in D minor for unaccompanied violin by Bach.

8 Variations of a Waltz Theme by Diabelli, Opus 120.

9 Variations on a Nursery Theme.

10 Fantasia on a Theme of Thomas Tallis.

Seven

Supply the most frequently used **Christian names of the following composers**. (One mark for each, maximum score 10)

1 Wagner

2 Berlioz

3 Elgar

7 Sibelius

8 Britten

9 Musorgsky

4 Mozart

5 Brahms

6 Verdi

10 Bizet

Eight

Below are some **personal details of composers' lives.** Which are true, and which false? (One mark for each correct answer, maximum score 10)

1 Wagner was Liszt's son-in-law.

2 Brahms married Schumann's widow.

3 Tchaikovsky was a homosexual.

4 J.S. Bach fathered twenty children.

5 Haydn was Beethoven's teacher.

6 George Sand was Chopin's wife.

7 Rossini invented the dish 'Tourne-dos Rossini'.

8 Paganini was never buried.

9 Percy Grainger was married on the stage of Carnegie Hall.

10 Saint-Saëns deserted his wife.

Nine

The following are **'scrambled' names of some famous musicians**. Fit the correct Christian name to each surname. Then supply the musical occupation of each person. (Two marks for each, maximum score 20)

1 Bruno Klemperer

2 Daniel Ashkenazy

8 John Barenboim

9 Janet Domingo

10 Fritz Landowska

3 Albert Williams

4 Placido Walter

5 Wanda Baker

6 Vladimir Kreisler

7 Otto Schweitzer

Ten

It would be too much to ask for the place of birth of the following composers, but can you give their **nationalities**? (One mark for each, maximum score 10)

1 Gluck

2 Nielsen

3 Wolf

4 Grieg

5 Szymanowski

6 Kodály

7 Albéniz

8 Pergolesi

9 Smetana

10 Villa-Lobos

Eleven

Below are some titles of **famous choral works**, plus a list of composers. Fit the correct composer to each work. (One mark for each correct combination, maximum score 10)

1	*The Dream of Gerontius*	Kodály
2	*Song of the High Hills*	Tippett
3	*The Creation*	Mendelssohn
4	*The St Matthew Passion*	Dvořák
5	*Belshazzar's Feast*	Handel
6	*Psalmus Hungaricus*	Elgar
7	*Judas Maccabaeus*	Haydn
8	*A Child of our Time*	Walton
9	*Elijah*	Bach
10	*St Ludmilla*	Delius

SECTION TWO

Twelve

A **mixed bag**, like those jumbo packs of foreign stamps one used to buy, **of 50 questions**. (One mark for each correct answer, maximum score 50)

1 Convert this quartet into a trio: Cortot, Thibaud, Primrose, Casals.
2 Who said of whom: 'Hats off, gentlemen — a genius!'?
3 Who said of whom: 'He has some very good moments, but some very bad quarters-of-an-hour!'?
4 'Herein is enshrined the soul of . . .'. On the title page of which composition would you find this mysterious and incomplete dedication?
5 In which language was the above quotation originally written?
6 Who dedicated a symphony to Napoleon but later removed the name and substituted: 'To the memory of a great man'?
7 Who wrote an unfinished opera on the Edgar Allan Poe story 'The Fall of the House of Usher'?
8 Which American composer ran a prosperous insurance business?
9 Beethoven 5 — Rachmaninov 4
Chopin 2 — Brahms 2
Schumann 1 — Wagner 0
Not a football score! So to what do the numbers refer?
10 Which tune does the *Symphonie Fantastique* by Berlioz have in common with Rachmaninov's Rhapsody on a Theme of Paganini?
11 Which famous play binds together the following composers: Berlioz, Prokofiev, Leonard Bernstein, Tchaikovsky?
12 Marlowe, Lenau and Goethe in literature, and Busoni, Gounod, Liszt and Berlioz (again!) in music, have given us portraits of which legendary character?
13 What is Beethoven's Opus 13?
14 Who founded the Hallé Orchestra?
15 This man founded the Royal Philharmonic Orchestra. Who is he?

16 Debussy's *La Mer* is a portrait of the sea. At which sea was he looking while writing it?
17 What would you do with a serpent?
18 What would you do with knackers?

19 Whose music was 'borrowed' for the score of the musical *Summer Song*?

20 Whose music was 'borrowed' for the score of the musical *Kismet*?

21 This man wrote the tune of the hymn 'Onward, Christian Soldiers'. Who was he?

22 Who wrote the tune for the carol 'Hark, the Herald Angels Sing'?

23 Who wrote the poem on which Richard Strauss based his opera *Salome*?

24 What was the real name of the English composer Peter Warlock?

25 How did he die?

26 Bach and Handel were both born in the same year. Which year?

27 How old was Schubert when he died?

28 Who wrote *Carmina Burana*?

29 Which Irish singer was made a Papal Count?

30 What is the other name given to Mendelssohn's Overture *The Hebrides*?

31 Bach's Toccata and Fugue in D minor; Beethoven's Symphony No. 6; Stravinsky's *Rite of Spring*; Tchaikovsky's *Nutcracker Suite*; Ponchielli's *Dance of the Hours*; Musorgsky's *Night on a Bare Mountain*; Schubert's *Ave Maria*. What have these works in common?

32 To whom was Schumann's Fantasia in C, Opus 17 dedicated?

33 The man in the picture below is Rimsky-Korsakov, one of 'the five'. Who were 'the five', and who were the other four?

34 Two of the following do not feature in Musorgsky's *Pictures At An Exhibition*. Which two? The Gnome; St Petersburg Square; The Hut on Fowl's Legs; The Old Gypsy; The Old Castle; Bydlo.

35 Which of the following is not one of Holst's *Planets*? Uranus; Pluto; Neptune; Venus; Mercury.

36 Which of the following is not a character in Schumann's *Carnival*? Chopin; Florestan; Paganini; Liszt; Pierrot.

37 Who is the odd-man-out: Pierre Fournier, Paul Tortelier, Arthur Grumiaux, Mstislav Rostropovich?

38 Who wrote *Three Pieces in the Shape of a Pear*?

39 Is it true that *Easter Parade* was written by Israel Baline?

40 Who was nicknamed 'Signor Crescendo'?

41 He was born, probably in Venice, about 1676. He died in Vienna in 1741. He wrote over 400 Concertos, was for many years director of music at a girls' orphanage, took Holy Orders, and was known as 'the red-headed priest'. Four of his best-known works comprise *The Seasons*. Who was he?

42 He was born in 1912, and has written a piece entitled *4'33"* in which the performer sits at the piano for four minutes and thirty-three seconds in silence. Who is he?

43 What do the following numbers have in common? 78, 45, 33⅓.

44 Handel in *Saul*, Walton in *Hamlet*, Chopin in B flat minor, Gounod for a marionnette . . . what?

45 Eugene, Leon, Sidonie and Marie . . . who?

46 Which of the following Dickens characters appears in Book II of Debussy's Preludes? The Artful Dodger; Mr. Pickwick; David Copperfield; Pip; Little Nell.

47 Which single word connects the following composers to the church? Palestrina; Mozart; Cherubini; Berlioz; Dvořák; Verdi; Fauré.

48 Why should an Australian singer, born in 1859, feature prominently on restaurant menus throughout the world?

49 His recording of *Vesti la giubba* made a unique contribution to the popularity of the early gramophones, and it is said that he earned almost £5,000 from record royalties. He died in 1921. Who was he?

50 Who played the part of the answer to the above question in a film biography made in 1951?

SECTION THREE

Thirteen

Identify the following composers from their photographs below. (One mark for each, maximum score 10)

1

2

3

4

5

6

7

The composer in question is sitting at the piano.

Fourteen

The following are the full titles of **works often known by subtitles or nicknames.** What are they? (One mark for each, maximum score 10)

Shostakovich

1 Chopin: Etude in A minor, Opus 25, No. 11.
2 Mozart: Symphony No. 38 in D, K. 504.
3 Schubert: Piano Quintet in A, D 667.
4 Beethoven: Sonata for violin and piano in A, Opus 47.
5 Shostakovich: Symphony No. 7, Opus 60.
6 Handel: Air and Variations from the 5th Harpsichord Suite.
7 Nielsen: Symphony No. 4, Opus 29.
8 Scriabin: Piano Sonata No. 9 in F major, Opus 68.
9 Mahler: Symphony No. 1 in D.
10 Stravinsky: Concerto for Clarinet and Orchestra (1945).

Fifteen

In which **operas** would you expect to find the following characters? (One mark for the opera, one mark for the composer, maximum score 20)

1 Radames (Captain of the Egyptian Guard).
2 King Marke (King of Cornwall).
3 Prince Orlofsky (a rich Russian).
4 Tonio (a Tyrolese peasant, in love with Marie).
5 Alvise Badoero (one of the heads of the State Inquisition).
6 Goro (a marriage broker).
7 Pluton (God of the Underworld, appearing on earth under the name of Aristée).
8 The Pretender Dimitri (also called Grigory).
9 Gennaro (a blacksmith).
10 The Dark Fiddler (rightful heir to the wood).

Sixteen

Composers have been writing **music for films** (with or without their knowledge!) since films began. Who wrote the scores for the following? (One mark for each, maximum score 10)

1 *Oliver Twist* (1948 version)

2 *Of Mice and Men* (1939)

3 *Scott of the Antarctic* (1948)

4 *La Ronde* (1950)

5 *On the Waterfront* (1954)

6 *Things to Come* (1936)

7 *Rififi* (1955)

8 *Alexander Nevsky* (1938)
9 *Far from the Madding Crowd* (1967)

10 *Hamlet* (1942)

Seventeen

What is (or are) the following? (One mark for each correct answer, maximum score 10)

1 A Toccata

2 A Nocturne

3 A Cadenza

4 A Passacaglia

5 A Jota

6 A Hautbois

7 A Triplet

8 A Volalise

9 A Dumka

10 An Acciaccatura

Eighteen

The path of success has not always been smooth for composers, and works later acknowledged as masterpieces have frequently received **disastrous reviews** in former days. Below are five such notices. For one mark identify the composer, for another the work under discussion. (Maximum score 10)

1 'If it were possible to imagine His Satanic Majesty writing an opera, ****** would be the sort of work he might be expected to turn out. After hearing it, we seem to have been assisting at some unholy rites, weirdly fascinating, but painful.
'The characters evoke no interest in the spectators; nay, more, they are eminently repulsive. It is another *La Traviata*, with the redeeming features which may be discovered in that libretto carefully eliminated. The heroine is an abandoned woman, destitute not only of any vestige of morality, but devoid of the ordinary feelings of humanity – soulless, heartless and fiendish. Indeed, so repulsive was the subject of the opera, that some of the best artists in Paris declined to be included in the cast. In the introduction we have a noisy, blatant theme, which starts off wildly without preface. Scarcely have we recovered from our surprise, when the bright key of A gives way to F, and a jovial march is heard.'
(*15 June 1878*)

2 'In his ****** (the composer) has succeeded in producing effects of the most horrible, hideous and disgusting sort. Among the special instruments in the score was the xylophone, the effect of which inevitably suggested (as doubtless intended) the clattering of the bones of skeletons. Another, and scarcely less hideous device, was the tuning of the first string of the solo violin half a note lower than usual, and the reiteration of the imperfect fifth many times in succession.'
(*3 June 1879*)

3 'Where Field smiles, ****** makes a leering grimace; where Field sighs, ****** groans; Field shrugs his shoulders, ****** arches his back like a cat; Field adds spice to his meal; ****** throws in a handful of pepper. If one were to hold Field's charming romances before a flawed mirror, so that every finer expression is exaggerated, then one would get ******'s handiwork.'
(*2 August 1833*)

4 'The (symphony) seemed to us as hard and as uninspired as upon its former hearing. It is mathematical music evolved with difficulty from an unimaginative brain. How it ever came to be honored with the title of

"THE TENTH SYMPHONY" is a mystery to us. This noisy, ungraceful, confusing and unattractive example of dry pedantry before the master-pieces of Schubert, Schumann, Mendelssohn, Gade, or even the reckless and over-fluent Raff! Absurd!
'All that we have seen and heard from ******'s pen abounds in headwork without a glimmer of soul.'
(*24 January 1878*)

5 'It has been supposed by many that music is an art which should be devoted largely to the exploitation of rare, subtle, higher emotions. The Italian composers today, however, believe differently. Their idea is that the promised land into which music should take us is the land of savagery, where lust, attempted violence, stabbing, shooting and suicide rule the day. 'These are the leading motives, the only motives, of this opera, and they seem even more gross and barbarous than they do in Sardou's play, because the action is more concentrated and the horrors follow one another more promptly. Were this opera the composer's first attempt, one might pardon it as the sin of a passionate musician sowing his wild oats. But he is forty three years old and this is his fifth opera.'
(*5 February 1901*)

Nineteen

Name the conductors, and then choose from the list below the orchestra with which each is most usually associated. (One mark for name, another for correct orchestra, maximum score 20)

The Los Angeles Philharmonic Orchestra

The Leipzig Gewandhaus Orchestra

Orchestre de la Suisse Romande

The Berlin Philharmonic Orchestra

The Concertgebouw, Amsterdam

The Royal Philharmonic Orchestra

The Philadelphia Orchestra

The Hallé Orchestra

The Chicago Symphony Orchestra

The London Symphony Orchestra

1

2

3

44

4

5

6

7

8

9

10

Twenty

'To see ourselves as others see us', said Robert Burns. How were some
famous composers viewed by those **relations and friends** around them?
Here are five varied reactions to great men. Which men? (One mark for
each, maximum score 5)

1 'One of the ideas that occupied his mind was the belief that he "could
never be cured at home", but must resign himself to the cure of some
physician. His wife made every effort to dissipate the phantoms and delu-
sions which haunted his fevered imagination. Hardly had she succeeded
when some new fancy would disturb his distracted brain. He declared
again and again that he was a sinner who did not deserve to be loved.
'Thus the unhappy master's agony increased, until at last, after a fortnight
of terrible struggle against his disease, he gave way, and his sufferings
drove him to a desperate step.
'He had left the house in his dressing-gown, with bare head, gone to the
bridge that spans the Rhine, and sought to end his misery by plunging
into the stream.'
(*Wilhelm Josef von Wasielewski, 1822–1896*)

2 'As the weeks went on the headaches (he) suffered did not arouse anything
more than quizzical comment until several months after their first occur-
rence, when a particularly severe attack prompted Leonore and Ira to
insist that (he) submit to a thorough physical checkup.
'This finally occurred on a Sunday morning, some six or seven weeks
before his last Sunday. When he came down and shuffled over in his beach
robe and sandals I called to him facetiously: "What did the doctors say?".
He laughed, as if in relief, and said: "Well, before they told me anything
they wanted to rule out the possibility of a brain tumor."
'With this final irony — in retrospect as in actuality — I reject the associa-
tion of ****** with anything but life.'
(*Oscar Levant, 1906–   *)

3 'With all his stern rigidity and moral equilibrium, the master has been not
alone one of the most generous of men, but one of the most loyal friends
and protectors. With the same austerity he has never let his right hand
know what his left has done.
'One instance we can mention — his kindness to his librettist Piave, who
for many years was ill, and incapacitated from working, and would have

been on the verge of starvation had (the composer) not come in oppor-
tunely and extended a helping hand. He not only aided Piave very early in
his illness, but during fifteen years gave the poet an annual allowance
from his own earnings, not only enough to keep him above want, but to
enable him to live in content and comfort.'
(*Blanche Roosevelt, 1853–1898*)

4 'I was about ten years old when Krumpholz took me to him. With what
joy and trembling I looked forward to the day when I was to see the great
man! I have a lively recollection of it still. My father, Krumpholz, and I set
out one winter day for the street called Tiefe Graben. We mounted five or
six storeys high to (the) apartment, and were announced by a rather dirty-
looking servant. In a very desolate room, with papers and articles of dress
strewn in all directions, bare walls, a few chests, hardly a chair except the
rickety one standing by the Walker piano (then the best make), there was
a party of six or eight people.
'(He) was dressed in a jacket and trousers of long, dark goat's hair, which
at once reminded me of the description of Robinson Crusoe I had just been
reading. He had a shock of jet-black hair (cut à la Titus) standing upright.
A beard of several days' growth made his naturally dark face still blacker.
I noticed also, with a child's quick observation, that he had cotton wool,
which seemed to have been dipped in some yellow fluid, in both ears.'
(*Karl Czerny, 1791–1857*)

5 '(He) never reached his natural growth. During his whole life, his health
was delicate. He was thin and pale, and though the form of his face was
unusual, there was nothing striking in his physiognomy but its extreme
variableness. The expression of his countenance changed every moment,
but indicated nothing more than the pleasure or pain which he experienced
at the instant.
'He was remarkable for a habit which is usually the attendant of stupidity.
His body was perpetually in motion; he was either playing with his hands,
or beating the ground with his foot. There was nothing extraordinary in
his other habits, except his extreme fondness for the game of billiards. He
had a table in his house, on which he played every day by himself, when
he had no one to play with. His hands were so habituated to the piano
that he was rather clumsy in everything else. At table he never carved, or
if he attempted to do so, it was with much awkwardness and difficulty.
'The same man, who, from his earliest age, had shown the greatest expan-

sion of mind in what related to his art, in other respects remained a child. He never knew how properly to conduct himself. The management of domestic affairs, the proper use of money, the judicious selection of his pleasures, and temperance in the enjoyment of them, were never virtues to his taste. The gratification of the moment was always uppermost with him.' (*Adolph Heinrich von Schlichtegroll, 1764–1822*)

Twenty-one

Another form of 'others seeing us'. Can you identify the subjects of the **cartoons and caricatures** below? (One mark for each, maximum score 10)

1

3

FRANCISCVS SCHREITET VBER DIE WASSER

4

5

54

Bravo, Kinder, bravo! so ist's ja eine Freude, hier oben zu sein, da krieg ich ja wieder Lust, etwas Neues zu komponiren!

7

8

9

10

Twenty-two

Some more **facts** (or are they?) **about musicians** for you to ponder. True or false? (One mark for each correct answer, maximum score 10)

1 Adolph Sax invented the saxophone.

2 John Philip Sousa invented the sousaphone.

3 William Glock invented the glockenspiel.

4 The pianist Paderewski was Prime Minister of Bulgaria.

5 César Cui was a general in the Russian army.

6 Balakirev worked as an official of the Russian railways.

7 Borodin worked as a chemist in a Russian university.

8 Henselt practised Bach's 48 Preludes and Fugues whilst reading the Bible at the same time.

9 The American statesman and writer Benjamin Franklin invented a glass harmonica.

10 Prince Carlo Gesualdo, an Italian composer famous for his madrigals, murdered his wife in 1590.

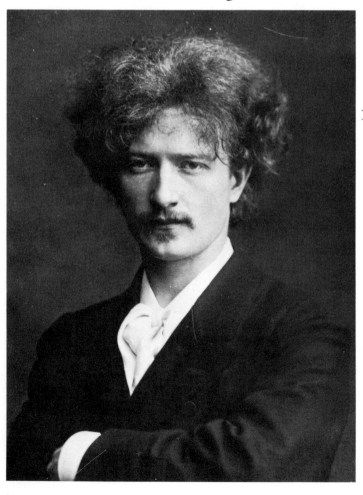

Twenty-three

Some more **operatic plots**, perhaps less well-known than the previous group. (As before, one mark for the opera, another for the composer, maximum score 20)

1 A gypsy girl is in love with a young man who is intending to marry another girl the very next day. In a small street in Granada there is a party with dancing, to celebrate the betrothal. At the party the gypsy upbraids the young man for his heartless deceit, and then drops dead at his feet from shock. Her grandmother and uncle curse the young man.

2 It is Windsor, during the reign of King Henry IV. Two ladies have received love letters from the same man. On visiting one of them the lover is surprised by the arrival of her husband, and is forced to hide in a linen basket. Later he avoids the same husband by dressing up as a woman. The final scene takes place in Windsor Forest where our hero conducts a liaison with both ladies of his choice, and two other characters dress up as fairies.

3 About 50BC, during the Roman occupation of Gaul, a High Priestess has fallen in love with a Roman Pro-Consul, and borne him two sons. Her lover betrays her with another woman, but later repents, and they both commit suicide by fire.

4 The son of the King of Clubs is ill and cannot be cured. Nothing can make the Prince laugh, until an old witch turns a somersault. The court jester cuts open some fruit in the desert, and out step two Princesses, who die of thirst. A third fruity Princess is saved by a bucket of water, but is later turned into a rat. The Princess is restored by a magician, and the culprits are saved by a witch.

5 The fiendish father of a Duke is ever with him, seeking his downfall. Banished from Normandy because of his evil deeds, the Duke arrives in thirteenth-century Sicily where he falls in love with a Princess. The Duke's father summons the spirits of nuns who were unfaithful to their holy vows in life and, enticed by their tempting, the Duke seizes a magic branch. The father's spell is finally broken by the Duke's foster sister.

6 In and around Richmond, about 1710, a lady is bored. As Maid of Honour to Queen Anne almost every man in court is in love with her, but she is indifferent to their advances. As a diversion she and her waiting maid visit Richmond Fair disguised as peasants, and flirt with a young farmer and his foster brother. Later it is discovered that the brother is, in fact, of noble

birth, which finally paves the way to a happy ending, uniting an Earl and Lady in a garden.

7   In Pressburg an exiled nobleman seeks refuge among some gypsies. Disguised as a gypsy, he saves the life of the Governor's daughter, but, shortly after, the child is kidnapped by a real gypsy. Twelve years later the little girl has grown up and fallen in love with the man who saved her life but, although he returns her love, he is loved in turn by the Queen of the Gypsies.
The Governor's daughter is accused of theft, but is saved from punishment when her father recognises a scar on her arm. The Queen of the Gypsies shoots herself by accident, and the young nobleman is finally free to marry the Governor's daughter.

8   Following a thunderclap, a girl is abducted by a dwarf, and her father promises her hand in marriage to anyone who will rescue her. Searching for her, a Knight finds a gigantic head, which can create a storm by its very breath. Under the head is a magic sword, with which the Knight slays the dwarf in a duel. The girl is awakened from a trance by a magic ring.

9   Round about 1650, in Bohemia, a forester is defeated by a peasant in a shooting competition. In order to win his superior's job (and the hand of his daughter in marriage) the defeated competitor must shoot again on the next day. Tempted by a fellow forester, the hero agrees to cheat, with the aid of seven magic bullets. At the shooting the seventh bullet kills the tempter himself.

10 We are in a large, round room. A staircase leads to a small door. There are seven other doors. There are no windows. A woman and a man enter and, on seeing the doors, the woman wishes to open them and air the castle. The man gives her the key to the first door, which discloses a torture chamber. The second door discloses an armoury. The third door discloses a treasury. The fourth door discloses a garden. The fifth door discloses a kingdom. The sixth door discloses tears. The seventh door discloses the woman's destiny.

Twenty-four

Below are photographs of ten musicians, some living, some dead. **Identify** each by name, and then, from the list below, pair each with **the instrument or occupation** with which he or she is most frequently associated. (One mark for each name, one for the instrument, maximum score 20)

Flute

Piano

Viola

Harpsichord

'Cello

Horn

Piano

Conductor

Guitar

Violin

1

2

3

4

5

6

7

8

9

10

Twenty-five

Below are the **plots of five well-known ballets**. For one mark give the title, for another the composer whose music is employed. (Maximum score 10)

1 The ballet opens with two players at a chessboard. One of the players (Love) supports a Red Knight to win the game, the other (Death) backs the Black Queen. The Knight falls in love with his adversary and so, at the moment of victory, cannot 'kill'. He is killed by the Queen and thus Death wins the game.

2 Subtitled 'The Girl With The Enamel Eyes', the story concerns a toy maker who creates a female doll which is so lifelike that two young people (who are in love with each other) believe her to be real.

3 Our heroine is married to a drunken cotton farmer. She denounces him to her fellow workers on the collective farm and in a fit of anger he attacks her and sets fire to the cotton. She is saved at the last moment by the Red Army Patrol. The husband is exiled and the woman freed to marry the Patrol Commander.

4 The women of a harem persuade the Chief Eunuch to admit men to visit them in the Shah's absence. During the orgy which follows the Shah returns unexpectedly and orders the execution of the male slaves and the women, among whom is his favourite wife.

5 A young girl is in love with a peasant boy who is, in reality, a nobleman in disguise, and betrothed to another. On discovering the truth she dies, driven mad by her grief, but returns as a spirit to save her lover from other spirits seeking to destroy him.

Twenty-six

Which composers or musicians **died under the following tragic and unusual circumstances**? (One mark for each correct answer, maximum score 10)

1 Complications after being knocked down by a bus.

2 Complications after being stung by a wasp.

3 Crushed under a falling bookcase.

4 Falling off a bicycle.

5 Shot in error by an American sentry.

6 As the result of banging himself on the foot with a stick whilst conducting.

7 Playing the Grieg Piano Concerto in Carnegie Hall.

8 Swimming to save his wife when the SS *Sussex* was torpedoed in the English Channel.

9 Awarded the Military Cross and killed, aged thirty-one, in 1916, fighting on the Somme.

10 Shot himself as the result of an unfortunate love affair.

Twenty-seven

Below are a few biographical notes on four famous musicians. If you can **guess the personality** in question from reading section A alone, score 10 marks. Guessing by section B scores 5. Otherwise continue to section C, for which a correct guess scores 1. (Maximum score 40)

1 *Section A*
Born Kiev, 1904.
Teacher: Felix Blumenfeld.
Berlin début 1925.
American début 1928, playing Tchaikovsky with the New York Philharmonic Orchestra, conducted by Sir Thomas Beecham.

Section B
Pianist.
Father-in-law: Toscanini.
Repertoire: mostly romantic music, but also celebrated for interpretation of Scriabin.

Section C
Renowned for remarkable technique.
Retired from platform, February 1953. Reappeared Carnegie Hall, 9 May 1965.
Famous for piano transcriptions of *Stars and Stripes* by Sousa, and variations on themes from Bizet's *Carmen*.
Christian name: Vladimir.

2 *Section A*
Born Recarati, 20 March 1890.
Teacher: Enrico Rosati.
Début 14 October 1914 in *La Gioconda*.
Appeared in Rome in 1916, and at La Scala, Milan, in 1918.

Section B
International stardom following début at New York Metropolitan, 26 November 1920.
Vocal characteristics: ease of delivery, natural phrasing and expression, warmth of tone. Sometimes criticised for lapses of taste and 'sentimentality'.
Supreme in Italian songs.

Section C
Tenor.
Acclaimed as successor to Caruso.
Also called the Greatest Tenor in the World.
Died 1957.
Christian name: Beniamino.

3 *Section A*
Born Vilna, 1901.
Teachers: Elias Malkin, then Leopold Auer.
Soloist, aged thirteen, at Berlin Philharmonic Concerts, conducted by Nikisch.
American début at Carnegie Hall, 27 October 1917.

Section B
Musical Times (London) June 1920: 'His ease is astonishing, and the way in which even in the most difficult passages he never scrapes nor scratches is all but unparalleled. His tone is strong and pure, like that of a high soprano rather than of a mezzo-soprano'.
Violinist.
Has composed popular tunes under the *nom de plume* Jim Hoyl.

Section C
Appeared in three films: *They Shall Have Music, Melody of Youth, Carnegie Hall.*
Settled in the USA.
Dedicatee of Walton Concerto.
Christian name: Jascha.

4 *Section A*
Born 2 December 1923 in New York.
Original name: Kalogeropoulou.
Début 1938.
Married 1947.

Section B
First Italian appearance: Verona in *La Gioconda* (1947).
Covent Garden début: 1952 (*Norma*).
Excelled in *bel canto* works – Donizetti, Cherubini, Bellini, and did much to revive interest in them.

Section C
Dramatic Soprano. Voice sometimes criticised for shrillness on high notes and excessive vibrato.
One-time companion of shipping millionaire.
Retired end of '60s to concentrate on teaching.
Died 1977.
Christian name: Maria.

Twenty-eight

Identify the composers who are the subjects of the statues and monuments shown below. (One mark for each, maximum score 10)

1

2

3

4

5

8

9

10

Twenty-nine

Some rather more difficult **'scrambled' names of musicians,** old and new.
As before, one mark for unscrambling, one mark for identifying occupation.
(Maximum score 20)

1 Hans Furtwängler

2 Luisa De Larrocha

3 Itzhak Ysaÿe

4 Nicanor Nikisch

5 Wilhelm Hotter

6 Arturo Benedetti Tetrazzini

7 Eugène Debost

8 Arthur Perlman

9 Alicia Zabeleta

10 Michel Michelangeli

Thirty

A friend of yours has heard five pieces of music which have particularly caught his attention, but, being something of a layman, he can't remember the titles. Can you identify the title and composer for him in each case? (One mark for each correct title, one mark for the composer, maximum score 10)

1 'It was quite short, no more than about five minutes long, and it was played by an orchestra, although the audience joined in at the end. It started with a sort of busy bit played on the strings and then gradually led up to quite a climax. Then there was a quiet, rather noble tune, and that led back to the busy bit being repeated all over again. Finally the orchestra played the noble tune again, and this time the audience joined in, singing words I couldn't quite catch, but it seemed to be something about the British Empire.'

2 'I heard this piece at a piano recital, and it was the last one the pianist played. The rhythm was quite firm and stately, but it also had a rhapsodic feel to it and every now and then it was interspersed with other episodes and one or two large scales — rushing up from the bottom of the keyboard to the top. What really interested me was the middle section. The pianist started playing a pattern of octaves in his left hand in very rapid groups of four, and over this drumming bass he then played another tune in short, sharp chords. The whole of this got louder and louder, working up to a furious climax, and as it finished the pianist played about twelve loud chords and then repeated the whole sequence. The piece ended with the main tune I'd first heard. It must be very tiring to play.'

3 'This much I do know, because I saw it on television, and that is there was a solo violinist playing with an orchestra. It began with the orchestra alone, and the opening was very quiet and lyrical. This became impassioned quite quickly and after about a minute the soloist began with a full version of the theme the orchestra had played only in fragments. This first theme the violin played haunted me through the whole movement, and later on it was taken up by the massed strings with some glorious "rat-a-tat-tat" brass interpolations added, quite loud and most thrilling. Shortly after, the violinist returned to the same tune yet again, in a very difficult passage when he played the theme on the top strings and accompanied himself by bouncing the bow back and forth on the lower ones. During this the orchestra just played short chords. Later on the soloist played all alone, without the orchestra, the same theme again, but differently arranged. I think it must be called the "main" theme! After that I had to go out

to my night shift, but my daughter remembers hearing someone say that the piece was turned down by the man it was written for and it was three years before someone else gave the first performance in Vienna.'

4 'I asked someone else about this the other day. I told them that it was an orchestra, although quite a small one, playing a piece that was in three separate sections. A fast one, then a sort of stately dance, and then a faster one still. My friend said these were called movements, and that the piece was probably a symphony. I don't think he can have been right because I always thought symphonies were quite serious things and this one was really ridiculous. In the middle movement the musicians played notes which sounded like bird calls, on different pipes. I'm sure I heard a cuckoo, and a duck, and there was a silver pipe with water in it. There was also a silly trumpet, that only seemed to be able to play one note, and a child's drum. In the first and last movements there was a rattle, and a triangle. When the piece came near the conclusion everyone started repeating the music faster and faster, over and over again. They all seemed to be enjoying themselves no end, but I thought it was rather silly — especially if it was supposed to be a symphony.'

5 'Well, naturally I recognised the main tune right away. It was our own (British) National Anthem, but I thought the way it was treated was disgraceful, without any respect at all. The piece started with the orchestra playing fragments of it, like fanfares and then, after the xylophone joined in, the orchestra played "God Save The Queen" quietly, and rather respectfully. However, this didn't last long and there then followed a series of variations on the tune, all of a rather irreverent nature. To be honest I was glad the whole thing didn't last for much more than seven minutes.'

Thirty-one

Below are five manuscripts, in other words examples of composers' 'musical handwriting'. Can you **identify the composer** in each case, **and also the sort of work** (symphony, piano concerto), if not the title of the specific piece? I have provided an extra clue in each case. (One mark for composer, one mark for category of work, maximum score 10)

1 You may not speak Italian but there are other very helpful verbal indications.

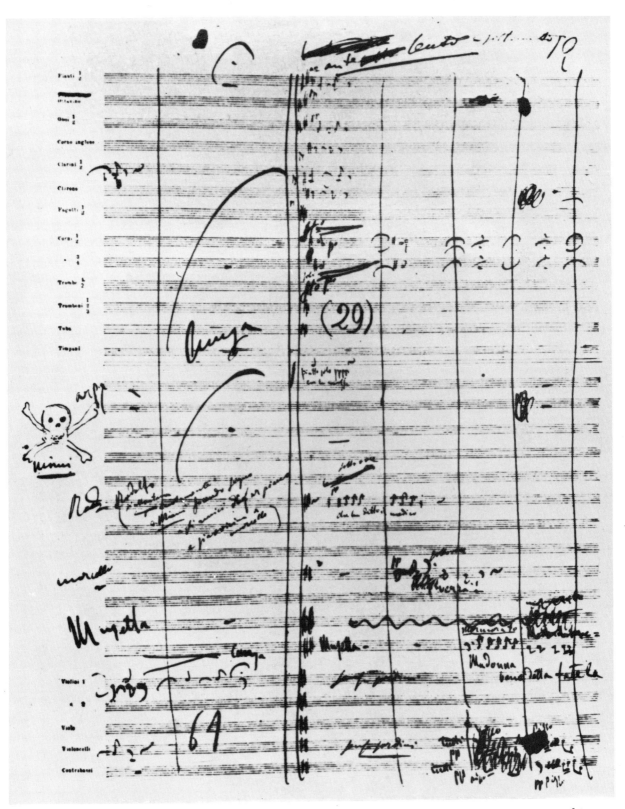

2 *Left* It's the opening of the work, and the composer's title is a useful clue.

3 *Above* This composer is something of a doodler, and there are vital names somewhere.

4 The generally chaotic state of the manuscript should tell you something
about the man himself if not the work.

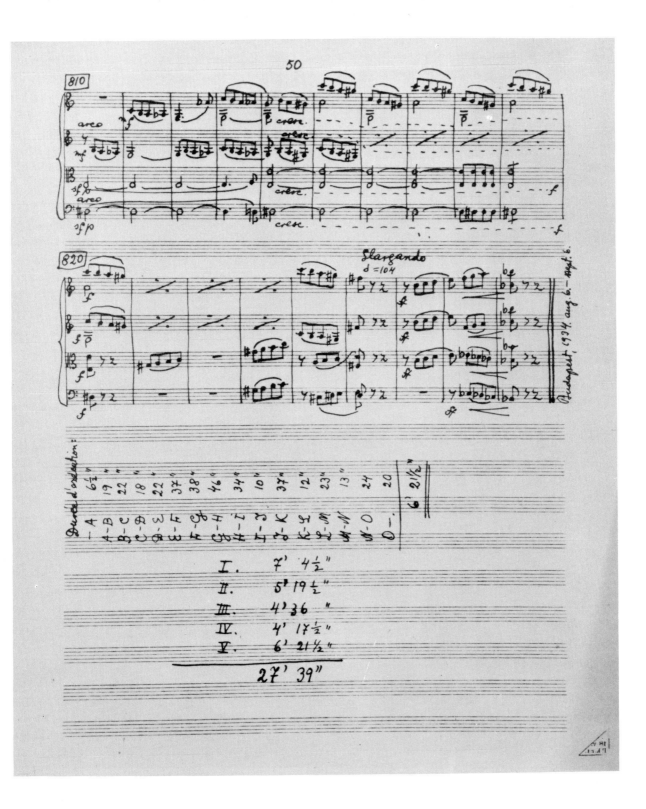

5 What a contrast to the one before! Where and when will tell you as much as what, if you don't read music.

Thirty-two

The **Christian names** of these composers are rather more difficult. (One mark for each, maximum score 10)

1 Balakirev

2 Bellini

3 Donizetti

4 Khachaturian

5 Palestrina

6 Cherubini

7 Dvořák

8 Buxtehude

9 Scriabin

10 Massenet

Thirty-three

Below are ten excerpts from operatic arias or songs, some in their original language, some not. **Identify the opera or song title** in each case, and then name the composer. (One mark for opera or song title, one for the composer, maximum score 20)

1 *I must go down to the sea again,*
   To the lonely sea and the sky,

2 *Vesti la giubba e la faccia infarina.*

3 *Who rides so late through night and wind?*
   It is the father with his child;
   He holds the boy safely in his arms,
   He grasps him surely, he keeps him warm.

4 *M'appari tutto amor*
   Il mio sguardo l'incontrò . . .

5 *Mon coeur s'ouvre à ta voix, comme s'ouvrent les fleurs*
   Aux baisers de l'aurore!

6 *My verses would fly, soft and frail towards your garden so fine,*
   If my verses had wings as a bird does.

7 *La fleur que tu m'avais jetée,*
   Dans ma prison m'était restée;

8 *There once was a Vilia, a fair mountain sprite,*
   She danced on the hill in the still of the night.
   A huntsman came by who was comely and tall,
   His horse for to graze by the cool waterfall.

9 *Che gelida manina, se la lasci riscaldar.*

10 *We have just seen the bull, three boys and three girls;*
   the weather was lovely on the lawn, where we were dancing a bolero
   to the sound of castanets;
   tell me, neighbour, if I look nice,
   and if my skirt fits well this morning;
   do you like my figure? Ah!

Thirty-four

The following are **composers' descriptions of their own music** Name the composer and work in each case. (One mark for each, maximum score 20)

1 'I am particularly desirous that there should be no misunderstanding about this work. There are no contrasts, and there is practically no invention, save the plan and the manner of execution. Before its first performance, I issued a warning to the effect that what I had written was a piece lasting seventeen minutes and consisting wholly of "orchestral tissue without music" – of one long, very gradual crescendo. I have carried out exactly what I intended, and it is for listeners to take it or leave it.'

2 'The typical English country garden is not often used to grow flowers in it; it is more likely to be a vegetable plot. So you can think of turnips as I play it.'

3 'I have grown accustomed to composing in our garden. . . . Today, or tomorrow, I am going to start dreaming there. ****** follows the play closely. At the end, after everything has been satisfactorily settled and the principal players have joyfully left the stage, the elves follow them, bless the house, and disappear with the dawn.'

4 'In the work under consideration, I endeavour to arrest attention by the opening theme. These three notes, proclaimed in unison in treble and bass, should boom solemnly and portentously. After this introduction the three-note melody runs through the first section of twelve bars, and counter to it, in both clefs, runs a contrasted melody in chords. The three notes of the first theme are not struck too loudly but with sufficient force to make the tones carry through.
'In the agitated section the melody in the right is carried by the first note in each group. The player must accommodate his pace to his technical ability. He must not hurry the passage beyond his capacity to make the melody stand out.
'The repetition of the first movement in doubled octaves calls for all the force the player is capable of. It will be safer to take this passage even a trifle more slowly than at the opening, and above all have regard for the evenness of the decrescendo.'

5 '****** describes the tragedy of a woman caught between two worlds, a world of reality which she cannot wholly comprehend, and a supernatural world in which she cannot believe. Baba has no scruples in cheating her clients, until something happens which she herself has not prepared. This

insignificant incident shatters her self-assurance, and drives her almost insane with rage.'

6 'A general description of the feelings which the sight of the Bohemian countryside conjures up. From nearly all sides a song both gay and melancholy rings out full of fervour from the groves and the meadows. The woodlands (horn solo) and the gay fertile lowlands of the Elbe and many, many other parts – everything is remembered in a hymn of praise. Everyone may imagine what he chooses when hearing this work – the poet has the field open to him, all he has to do is follow the composition in detail.'

7 'In *our* symphony there is a programme. That is, it is possible for me to outline in words what it attempts to express, and to you, to you alone, I want and am able to communicate the meaning of the whole, as well as of the separate sections.
'The introduction contains the germ of the entire symphony, without question its central idea: this is Fate, the fatal force that prevents our striving for happiness from succeeding. The second movement of the symphony expresses another phase of longing. This is the melancholy feeling that suffuses you towards evening when you are sitting alone, weary from work. A host of memories appears. And you are sad because so much is already past. The third movement expresses no definite sensations. The soul is neither happy nor sad. The fourth movement. If you cannot discover reasons for happiness in yourself, look at others. Get out among the people. Upbraid yourself and do not say that all the world is sad. Life is bearable after all.'

8 'Six dreadful ****** composed by me at the country place of my friend Triossi when I was at the most infantile age, not even having taken a lesson in accompaniment, the whole composed and copied out in three days and performed by Triossi, double-bass, his cousin, first violin, the latter's brother, violoncello – who played like dogs – and the second violin by me myself, who was not the least doggish, by God.'

9 'All that I could hope to do was to reflect the Mexico of the tourists, and that is why I thought of the ******. Because in that "hot spot" one felt, in a very natural and unaffected way, a close contact with the Mexican people. It wasn't the music I heard, but the spirit that I felt there, which attracted me. Something of that spirit is what I hope to have put into my music.'

10 'I first became conscious of thematic ideas in the summer of 1911. Reaching Switzerland in the fall, I rented a house for my family and began to work. The entire ****** was written in a tiny room of this house, whose only furniture was a small upright piano, which I kept muted, a table and two chairs. 'That the first performance was attended by a scandal must be known to everybody; I was unprepared for the explosion myself. Mild protests against the music could be heard from the beginning — then when the curtain opened on a group of knock-kneed "Lolitas" jumping up and down, the storm broke. I left the hall in a rage. I was sitting on the right, near the orchestra, and I remember slamming the door. I have never been that angry. The music was so familiar to me, I loved it, and I could not understand why people who had not yet heard it wanted to protest in advance.'

SECTION FOUR

Thirty-five

Now to finish off, and **for** those **musical wizards** who have been saying 'It's all too easy!', here are some real stinkers. Most people will not only not know the answers, they probably won't even care. But for those who do — either way! — one mark for each. (Maximum score 30)

1 For whom, and for what 'sinister' purpose, did Ravel write his Concerto in D major?
2 Who was 'Old Arpeggio'?
3 What patriotic song does Schumann quote in his Opus 26?
4 Who wrote *Fra Diavolo, ou L'Hotellerie de Terracine*?
5 Who invented the metronome?
6 Who arranged a Bach Toccata and Fugue for orchestra under the name Klenovsky?
7 Which violinist (hearing the young Heifetz play) exclaimed 'Phew! It's hot in here.'?
8 Which pianist replied: 'Not for pianists!'?
9 Under which omnibus title does Liszt portray two saints named Francis?
10 Who wrote *The Song of the Flea*?
11 Who wrote *Babar le petit Eléphant*?
12 Who wrote *The Cunning Little Vixen*?
13 What was the year of Wagner's birth?
14 In which key is the Brahms Violin Concerto?
15 In which key is the 5th Symphony of Sibelius?
16 What was the year of Saint-Saëns's death?
17 Who is the soloist in this photo?

18 Who is the conductor?

19 Who is the composer/conductor in this photo?

Name the composers in the four following pictures.

20 Name the 'cellist in this photo.

21

23   24

25 Name three pieces from the suite *Iberia* by Albéniz.

26 Name the lady born in Paris in 1857, who died in Monte Carlo in 1944, and of whom Ambrose Thomas said: 'This is not a woman composer but a composer woman.'

27 Which composer went deaf in 1874 and died insane?

29 What do Michael Rabin, Claudio Arrau and Elizabeth Taylor have in common?

29 What is the Opus number of Chopin's Impromptu in A flat?

30 With which well-known composer did Ravel study composition?

Answers

Section One

QUIZ ONE, page 8: Composers' Portraits

1 Handel.
2 Haydn.
3 Mozart.
4 Rossini.
5 Schubert.
6 Berlioz.
7 Chopin.
8 Verdi.
9 Tchaikovsky.
10 Debussy.

QUIZ TWO, page 11: Potted Opera Plots (I)

1 *La Bohème*, Puccini.
2 *The Magic Flute*, Mozart.
3 *La Traviata*, Verdi.
4 *Der Rosenkavalier*, Strauss.
5 *Billy Budd*, Britten.
6 *Carmen*, Bizet.
7 *Fidelio*, Beethoven.
8 *Porgy and Bess*, Gershwin.
9 *Die Meistersinger von Nürnberg*, Wagner.
10 *Cavalleria Rusticana*, Mascagni.

QUIZ THREE, page 12: Actors as Composers

1 Richard Chamberlain — Tchaikovsky — *The Music Lovers*.
2 Clifton Webb — John Philip Sousa — *Stars and Stripes Forever*. (English title: *Marching Along*).
3 Stewart Grainger — Paganini — *The Magic Bow*.
4 Richard Tauber — Schubert — *Blossom Time*.
5 Dirk Bogarde — Liszt — *Song Without End*.
6 Cornel Wilde — Chopin — *A Song To Remember*.
7 Don Ameche — Stephen Foster — *Swanee River*.
8 Wilfred Lawson — Handel — *The Great Mr. Handel*.
9 José Ferrer — Sigmund Romberg — *Deep In My Heart*.
10 Cary Grant — Cole Porter — *Night and Day*.

QUIZ FOUR, page 15: Musical Terms (I)

1 Half voice.
2 Slow.
3 Diminishing (in volume).
4 Sliding (from one note to another).
5 Detached (opposite of legato).
6 Fast.
7 Little.
8 Like a harp (notes of a chord played one after another).
9 Follows.
10 Dashing, brilliant, with great spirit.

QUIZ FIVE, page 16: Photographs of Musicians

1 John Ogdon.
2 Leopold Stokowski.
3 Artur Rubinstein.
4 Yehudi Menuhin.
5 Sir Adrian Boult.
6 Rosalyn Tureck.
7 Sir Benjamin Britten.
8 Julian Bream.
9 Claudio Abbado.
10 Kyung-Wha Chung.

QUIZ SIX, page 19: Variations on a Theme
1 Ravel.
2 Rachmaninov.
3 Brahms.
4 Hindemith.
5 Britten.
6 Liszt.
7 Busoni — or, for the left hand, Brahms. (One mark for either)
7 Beethoven.
9 Dohnányi.
10 Vaughan Williams.

QUIZ SEVEN, page 20: Composers' Christian Names (I)
1 Richard (Wilhelm Richard) (Wagner).
2 Hector (Louis Hector) (Berlioz).
3 Edward (Elgar).
4 Wolfgang Amadeus (Mozart).
5 Johannes (Brahms).
6 Giuseppe (Giuseppe Fortunino Francesco) (Verdi).
7 Jean (Sibelius) (Real names: Johan Julian Christian).
8 Benjamin (Edward Benjamin) (Britten).
9 Modeste (Modeste Petrovich) (Musorgsky).
10 Georges (Bizet) (Original names: Alexandre César Léopold).

QUIZ EIGHT, page 21: Private Lives
1 True. Cosima, daughter of Liszt and the Countess d'Agoult, married Richard Wagner.
2 False. Brahms was a pupil of Schumann's and a friend of his widow Clara, but remained a bachelor all his life.
3 True.
4 True. Bach fathered a total of 20 children by two wives.
5 True. Beethoven did take lessons from Haydn.
6 False. George Sand was Chopin's close companion but never his wife.
7 True. Rossini was a great *bon viveur* and was the creator of this famous dish of fillet steak, paté and truffles.
8 False, although Paganini *was* refused burial in consecrated ground, as a result of fostering the rumour that he was in league with the devil.
9 False. Grainger was married on the stage of the Hollywood Bowl.
10 True. Saint-Saëns walked out on his wife, never to return.

QUIZ NINE, page 22: Scrambled Names (I)
1 Otto Klemperer, Conductor.
2 Vladimir Ashkenazy, Pianist.
3 John Williams, Guitarist.
4 Bruno Walter, Conductor.
5 Janet Baker, Mezzo-Soprano.
6 Fritz Kreisler, Violinist.
7 Albert Schweitzer, Organist.
8 Daniel Barenboim, Pianist (more recently Conductor).
9 Placido Domingo, Tenor.
10 Wanda Landowska, Harpsichordist.

QUIZ TEN, page 23: Composers' Nationalities
1 Christoph Willibald von Gluck was German.
2 Carl August Nielsen was Danish.
3 Hugo Wolf was Austrian.
4 Edvard Hagerup Grieg was Norwegian.
5 Karol Szymanowski was Polish.
6 Zoltán Kodály was Hungarian.
7 Isaac Albéniz was Spanish.
8 Giovanni Battista Pergolesi was Italian.
9 Bedřich Smetana was Czech (Bohemian).
10 Heitor Villa-Lobos was Brazilian.

1 *The Dream of Gerontius* — Elgar.
2 *Song of the High Hills* — Delius.
3 *The Creation* — Haydn.
4 *The St Matthew Passion* — Bach.
5 *Belshazzar's Feast* — Walton.
6 *Psalmus Hungaricus* — Kodály.
7 *Judas Maccabaeus* — Handel.
8 *A Child of our Time* — Tippett.
9 *Elijah* — Mendelssohn.
10 *St Ludmilla* — Dvořák.

Section Two

QUIZ TWELVE, page 26: Mixed Bag

1 Omit viola player William Primrose. Alfred Cortot, Jacques Thibaud and Pablo Casals were a celebrated trio.
2 Schumann of Chopin, commenting on the latter's variations on *La Ci Darem Lo Mano*.
3 Rossini of Wagner.
4 This 'enigmatic' dedication is found on the score of Elgar's Violin Concerto in B minor.
5 It was written in Spanish.
6 Beethoven — the Symphony No. 3 in E flat (Eroica).
7 Debussy.
8 Charles Ives, and he wrote a book on the subject: *A Manual of Insurance*.
9 The numbers refer to how many Piano Concertos each composer wrote.
10 The Dies Irae from the *Requiem Mass*.
11 They all wrote music for or about Shakespeare's *Romeo and Juliet*. (Bernstein's *West Side Story* is an updated version.)
12 Faust.
13 Beethoven's Opus 13 is the Piano Sonata No. 8 in C minor (The Pathétique).
14 The Hallé Orchestra was founded by Sir Charles Hallé.
15 The Royal Philharmonic Orchestra was founded by Sir Thomas Beecham. (He also founded the London Philharmonic Orchestra.)
16 The English Channel — seen from a hotel in Eastbourne.
17 You would blow it. The serpent (or Snake Tube) was a bass cornett, developed during the sixteenth century.
18 Strike them. They are a sort of early drum.
19 Dvořák's music is the basis for *Summer Song*.
20 Borodin's music is the basis for *Kismet*.
21 Sir Arthur Sullivan (who also wrote *The Lost Chord*).
22 Mendelssohn.
23 Oscar Wilde (but the poem was translated into German by Hedwig Lachmann).
24 Philip Heseltine was Warlock's real name. He also wrote under the name of Rab Noolas. (Try it backwards — or, rather, forwards.)
25 He committed suicide in London in 1930.
26 Both Bach and Handel were born in 1685. (So was the great harpsichord composer Domenico Scarlatti.)
27 Franz Schubert died aged 31 (1797–1828).
28 Carl Orff. This cantata, based on poems about love, drink and pleasure, was first performed in 1937.
29 John McCormack (1884–1945).
30 Fingal's Cave.
31 All were featured in Walt Disney's film *Fantasia*.
32 Schumann's Fantasia in C is dedicated to Liszt, who was raising money to build a monument to Beethoven in Bonn.
33 A group of Russian composers of the latter half of the nineteenth century. Their names are Balakirev, Borodin, Cui, Musorgsky and Rimsky-Korsakov.

34 Odd-men-out are St Petersburg Square and The Old Gypsy.
35 Pluto does not feature in Holst's suite *The Planets*.
36 Liszt was not present at Schumann's *Carnival*.
37 The Belgian-born violinist Arthur Grumiaux is the odd-man-out. All the others are 'cellists.
38 Erik Satie (1866–1925). Satie specialised in eccentric titles, as well as owning a large collection of umbrellas and handkerchiefs!
39 Yes, it is true. Israel Baline is the real name of Irving Berlin.
40 Rossini, after his habit of writing extended crescendi.
41 Vivaldi.
42 John Cage.
43 They are all playing speeds (revolutions per minute) for gramophone records.
44 Funeral Marches.
45 All are Christian names of members of the celebrated Goossens family.
46 It is Mr Pickwick who appears in Book II of Debussy's Preludes.
47 Requiem.
48 Because Peach Melba and Melba Toast are named after Dame Nellie Melba.
49 Caruso.
50 Mario Lanza.

Section Three

QUIZ THIRTEEN, page 30: Composers' Photographs

1 Massenet.
2 Puccini.
3 Sousa.
4 Bruckner.
5 Gershwin.
6 Walton.
7 Rachmaninov.
8 Vaughan Williams.
9 Stravinsky.
10 Ravel.

QUIZ FOURTEEN, page 33: Nicknamed Compositions

1 Chopin: The Winter Wind Study.
2 Mozart: The Prague Symphony.
3 Schubert: The Trout Quintet.
4 Beethoven: The Kreutzer Sonata.
5 Shostakovich: The Leningrad Symphony.
6 Handel: The Harmonious Blacksmith Variations.
7 Nielsen: The Inextinguishable Symphony.
8 Scriabin: The Black Mass Sonata.
9 Mahler: The Titan Symphony.
10 Stravinsky: The Ebony Concerto.

QUIZ FIFTEEN, page 33: Operatic Characters

1 *Aida*, Verdi.
2 *Tristan and Isolde*, Wagner.
3 *Die Fledermaus*, Johann Strauss.
4 *The Daughter of the Regiment*, Donizetti.
5 *La Gioconda*, Ponchielli.
6 *Madame Butterfly*, Puccini.
7 *Orpheus in the Underworld*, Offenbach.
8 *Boris Godunov*, Musorgsky.
9 *The Jewels of the Madonna*, Wolf-Ferrari.
10 *A Village Romeo and Juliet*, Delius.

QUIZ SIXTEEN, page 34: Film Scores

1 Arnold Bax.
2 Aaron Copland.
3 Ralph Vaughan Williams. (Later expanded by the composer into his 7th Symphony, 1953.)
4 Oscar Straus.
5 Leonard Bernstein.
6 Arthur Bliss.
7 Georges Auric.
8 Serge Prokofiev.
9 Richard Rodney Bennett.
10 Sir William Walton.

QUIZ SEVENTEEN, page 40: Musical Terms (II)

1 A brilliant show piece (to demonstrate 'touch').
2 A night piece — usually soft and gentle, but sometimes with impassioned episodes.
3 A passage in which a soloist is given the opportunity to demonstrate showmanship — often difficult, sometimes written out by the composer, sometimes improvised.
4 An Italian dance in triple time, written on a ground bass.
5 Another dance, after the waltz style, originating in Northern Spain.
6 An oboe.
7 Three notes played in the time of two.
8 A wordless song.
9 A Russian lament.
10 A 'crushed note' played very quickly before the main note that follows it.

QUIZ EIGHTEEN, page 41: Disastrous Reviews

1 *Carmen* by Bizet. (*Music Trade Review*, London.)
2 *Danse Macabre* by Saint-Saëns. (*London Daily News*.)
3 Nocturnes, Opus 9 by Chopin. (Ludwig Rellstab, *Iris in the Realm of Music*, Berlin.)
4 Symphony No. 1 by Brahms. (*Boston Gazette*.)
5 *Tosca* by Puccini. (*New York Evening Post*.)

QUIZ NINETEEN, page 43: Conductors and Their Orchestras

1 Eugene Ormandy — The Philadelphia Orchestra.
2 Sir John Barbirolli — The Hallé Orchestra.
3 Sir Thomas Beecham — The Royal Philharmonic Orchestra.
4 Sir George Solti — The Chicago Symphony Orchestra.
5 André Previn — The London Symphony Orchestra.
6 Kurt Masur — The Gewandhaus Orchestra.
7 Eduard Van Beinum — The Concertgebouw, Amsterdam.
8 Ernest Ansermet — Orchestre de la Suisse Romande.
9 Herbert Von Karajan — The Berlin Philharmonic Orchestra.
10 Zubin Mehta — The Los Angeles Philharmonic Orchestra.

QUIZ TWENTY, page 48: Composers by Their Contemporaries

1 Schumann.
2 George Gershwin.
3 Verdi.
4 Beethoven.
5 Mozart.

QUIZ TWENTY-ONE, page 51: Caricatures of Composers

1 Donizetti.
2 Verdi.
3 Liszt.
4 Paganini.
5 Mendelssohn.
6 Wagner.
7 Weber.
8 Offenbach.
9 Rubinstein (Anton).
10 Mahler.

QUIZ TWENTY-TWO, page 58: Facts — True or False?

All are true except numbers 3 and 4. Sir William Glock held an executive musical post with the British Broadcasting Corporation. Paderewski was Prime Minister of Poland, not Bulgaria.

QUIZ TWENTY-THREE, page 59: Potted Opera Plots (II)

1 *La Vida Breve*, Falla.
2 *The Merry Wives of Windsor*, Nicolai.
3 *Norma*, Bellini.
4 *The Love for Three Oranges*, Prokofiev.
5 *Robert Le Diable*, Meyerbeer.
6 *Martha*, Flotow.

7 *The Bohemian Girl*, Balfe.
8 *Russlan and Ludmilla*, Glinka.

9 *Der Freischütz*, Weber.
10 *Bluebeard's Castle*, Bartók.

QUIZ TWENTY-FOUR, page 61: Who Plays What?
1 Claudio Arrau – piano.
2 Lionel Tertis – Viola.
3 Dennis Brain – Horn.
4 Pablo Casals – 'Cello.
5 Andrés Segovia – Guitar.

6 Pinchas Zukerman – Violin.
7 James Galway – Flute.
8 Raymond Leppard – Conductor.
9 Dame Myra Hess – Piano.
10 George Malcolm – Harpsichord.

QUIZ TWENTY-FIVE, page 65: Potted Ballet Plots
1 *Checkmate*. Music by Arthur Bliss.
2 *Coppélia*. Music by Delibes.
3 *Gayaneh*. Music by Khachaturian.

4 *Scheherazade*. Music by Rimsky-Korsakov.
5 *Giselle*. Music by Adam.

QUIZ TWENTY-SIX, page 66: Unusual Deaths
1 César Franck, born 1822, died 1890.
2 Alban Berg, born 1855, died 1935.
3 Charles Valentin Alkan, born 1813, died 1888.
4 Ernest Chausson, born 1855, died 1899.
5 Anton von Webern, born 1833, died 1945.
6 Jean-Baptiste Lully, born 1632, died 1687.
7 Simon Barere, born 1896, died 1951.
8 Enrique Granados, born 1867, died 1916.
9 George Butterworth, born 1885, died 1916.
10 Jeremiah Clarke, born (about) 1660, died 1707.

QUIZ TWENTY-SEVEN, page 67: Musicians' Biographies
1 Horowitz.
2 Gigli.

3 Heifetz.
4 Callas.

QUIZ TWENTY-EIGHT, page 69: Composers' Statues
1 Handel.
2 J.S. Bach.
3 Haydn.
4 Mozart.
5 Beethoven.

6 Schubert.
7 Chopin.
8 Puccini.
9 Sullivan.
10 Grieg.

QUIZ TWENTY-NINE, page 72: Scrambled Names (II)
1 Wilhelm Furtwängler – Conductor.
2 Alicia De Larrocha – Pianist.
3 Eugène Ysaÿe – Violinist.
4 Arthur Nikisch – Conductor.
5 Hans Hotter – Baritone.

6 Luisa Tetrazzini – Soprano.
7 Michel Debost – Flautist.
8 Itzhak Perlman – Violinist.
9 Nicanor Zabeleta – Harpist.
10 Arturo Benedetti Michelangeli – Pianist.

QUIZ THIRTY, page 73: Layman's Musical Descriptions
1 *Pomp and Circumstance* March No. 1, Elgar.
2 Polonaise in A flat, Chopin.
3 Violin Concerto in D major, Tchaikovsky.
4 'Toy' Symphony in C, attributed to Haydn but in reality compiled by Mozart's father Leopold, with toys added by Michael Haydn, Joseph's brother. (Score one mark for any, or all, of these composers.)
5 Variations on 'America', Charles Ives. ('God Save the Queen' is also known as 'America' in the USA.)

QUIZ THIRTY-ONE, page 75: Composers' Musical Handwriting

1 Mozart: Opera, *Le Nozze di Figaro*.
2 Berlioz: First movement of the *Symphonie Fantastique*.
3 Puccini: Opera, *La Bohème*.
4 Beethoven: Piano Sonata in E major, Opus 109.
5 Bartók: String Quartet No. 5.

QUIZ THIRTY TWO, page 80: Composers' Christian Names (II)

1 Mily (Mily Alexeyevich) (Balakirev).
2 Vincenzo (Bellini).
3 Gaetano (Donizetti).
4 Aram (Aram Ilich) (Khachaturian).
5 Giovanni (Giovanni Pierluigi da) (Palestrina).
6 Maria (Maria Luigi Carlo Zenobio Salvatore) (Cherubini).
7 Antonín (Dvořák).
8 Diderik (Buxtehude).
9 Alexander (Alexander Nikolayevich) (Scriabin).
10 Jules (Émile Frédéric) (Massenet).

QUIZ THIRTY-THREE, page 81: Words of Arias and Songs

1 'Sea Fever' by John Ireland.
2 'On with the motley . . .' from *Pagliacci* by Leoncavallo.
3 'Erlkönig' by Schubert.
4 'She appeared to me full of love . . .' from *Martha* by Flotow.
5 'Softly awakes my heart' from *Samson et Dalila* by Saint-Saëns.
6 'Si mes vers avaient des ailes' by Reynaldo Hahn.
7 The Flower Song from *Carmen* by Bizet.
8 'Vilia' from *The Merry Widow* by Lehár.
9 'Your tiny hand is frozen' from *La Bohème* by Puccini.
10 *Les Filles de Cadiz* (The Girls of Cadiz) by Delibes.

QUIZ THIRTY-FOUR, page 82: Composers on Their Own Music

1 Ravel, on *Bolero*.
2 Grainger, on *Country Gardens*.
3 Mendelssohn, on *A Midsummer Night's Dream*.
4 Rachmaninov, on Prelude in C sharp minor.
5 Menotti, on *The Medium*.
6 Smetana, on *Má Vlast* (Fourth movement).
7 Tchaikovsky, on Symphony No. 4.
8 Rossini, on Six String Sonatas. (He wrote them aged 12.)
9 Copland, on *El Salón México*.
10 Stravinsky, on *The Rite of Spring*.

Section Four

QUIZ THIRTY-FIVE, page 86: Buff's Delight (?)

1 For Paul Wittgenstein, who lost his right arm in World War I. The clue 'sinister' refers to the title 'Concerto for The Left Hand'.
2 The pianist Thalberg (Liszt's great rival).
3 'Le Marseillaise' is quoted in Schumann's *Carnival Jest from Vienna*. (It was forbidden to play the 'Marseillaise' in Germany at the time.)
4 *Fra Diavolo, ou L'Hotellerie de Terracine* was written by Daniel François Esprit Auber. (This is a silly question for people who like long names and titles!)
5 Johann Nepomuk Maelzel invented the metronome.
6 Sir Henry Wood, founder of the Promenade Concerts.
7 Mischa Elman.
8 Leopold Godowsky.

9 Two Legends. (St Francis of Assisi Preaching to the Birds; St Francis of Paolo Walking on the Waves.)
10 Musorgsky. (An easy one for those losing heart!)
11 Poulenc.
12 Janáček.
13 Wagner was born in 1813.
14 The Brahms Violin Concerto is in D major.
15 Sibelius's Symphony No. 5 is in E flat.
16 Saint-Saëns died in 1921.
17 Russian pianist Emil Gilels.
18 Eugen Jochum.
19 Constant Lambert.
20 The young Pablo Casals.
21 Purcell.
22 Donizetti.
23 Bizet.
24 Holst.
25 *Iberia* consists of: Evocation; El Puerto; Fête-Dieu à Seville; Rondeña; Almería; Triana; El Albaicín; El Polo; Lavapies; Málaga; Jérez; Eritaña. So take your choice of any three.
26 Cécile Chaminade.
27 Smetana.
28 All featured in the Hollywood film *Rhapsody*. Taylor was the star, Arrau provided the piano soundtrack, Rabin the violin soundtrack.
29 29.
30 Fauré was Ravel's composition teacher at the Paris Conservatoire.